PERFECT
COMMUNICATION

Terry O'Brien is a best-selling author, columnist, consultant and motivational trainer. He is highly sought-after in the corporate as well as academic world, and has been training managers and providing counselling and consultancy over the past couple of decades. Author of hugely popular books on motivation, effective change and all that is 'un-Google-able', his writings focus on skill development and communication techniques. Terry O'Brien is a firm believer that 'infotainment' is a must for content to be effective, and his books are all about the three 'R's: Read, Record and Recall.

OTHER TITLES IN THE SERIES

Perfect Appraisal

Perfect Assertiveness

Perfect CV

Perfect Interview

Perfect Leader

Perfect Management Skills

Perfect Marketing

Perfect Meeting

Perfect Negotiation

Perfect People Skills

Perfect Personality

Perfect Presentation

Perfect Salesmanship

Perfect Strategy

Perfect Time Management

PERFECT
COMMUNICATION

Get it right every time

Terry O'Brien

RUPA

Published by
Rupa Publications India Pvt. Ltd 2017
7/16, Ansari Road, Daryaganj
New Delhi 110002

Sales centres:
Allahabad Bengaluru Chennai
Hyderabad Jaipur Kathmandu
Kolkata Mumbai

Copyright © Terry O'Brien 2017

The views and opinions expressed in this book are the
author's own and the facts are as reported by him/her which
have been verified to the extent possible, and the publishers
are not in any way liable for the same.

All rights reserved.
No part of this publication may be reproduced, transmitted,
or stored in a retrieval system, in any form or by any means,
electronic, mechanical, photocopying, recording or otherwise,
without the prior permission of the publisher.

ISBN: 978-81-291-4544-4

First impression 2017

10 9 8 7 6 5 4 3 2 1

Printed by Nutech Print Services, New Delhi

Typeset by Chetan Sharma

This book is sold subject to the condition that it shall not,
by way of trade or otherwise, be lent, resold, hired out, or otherwise
circulated, without the publisher's prior consent, in any form of
binding or cover other than that in which it is published.

Contents

Introduction		*vii*
1.	Speaking skills	1
2.	Writing skills	51
3.	Listening skills	91

Introduction

The word communication is derived from Latin words 'communis' and 'communicare' which mean 'commonality' and 'to make common', respectively. From the viewpoint of etymological depth, communication refers to sharing of information, knowledge or meaning. Therefore, communication may be broadly defined as the process of meaningful interaction among people.

A message is an attempt to engage in a two-way communication with the person on the other end. Two-way communication is when one person, the sender, transmits a message to another person, the receiver. When the receiver gets the message, they send back a response, acknowledging that the message was received. The model looks like this:

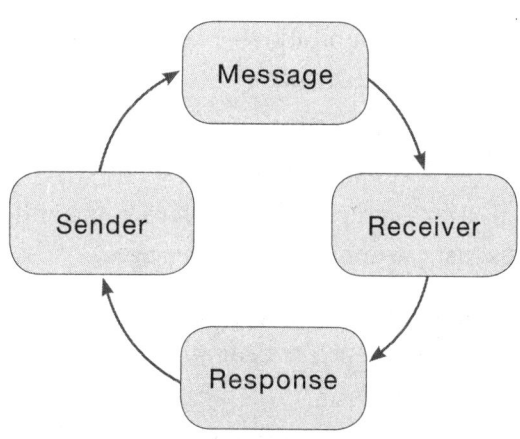

Two-way communication is essential in the business world. Messages are transmitted between employers, employees, customers and other stakeholders, and feedback is required to be certain that the message was received and understood. What matters most is 'response-ability'—the response is more important than the message.

We use 'communication' usually to mean speaking, writing or sending a message to another person. Communication is really much more than that. It involves a number of choices and decisions. In formal situations, our communication needs to be more effective and thus, we need to plan our communication.

What is communication? In simple terms, communication is simply the act of transferring information. There are various categories of communication and more than one may be used at a time.

The different categories of communication include:
- spoken or verbal communication—face-to-face, telephone, radio or television and other media.
- non-verbal communication—body language, gestures and how we dress or act.
- written communication—letters, emails, books, magazines, the Internet or other media.
- visualisation—graphs, charts, maps, logos and other visuals that can communicate messages.

Thus, it is important that we hone our speaking, writing and listening skills. *Perfect Communication* spells out the rudiments that make one an effective communicator in all these aspects. This book is based on the premise of experience and learning; it makes little claim to originality or depth.

Indeed, here is all you need to get it right every time!

Speaking Skills

These are the three 'S's that form the essence of speaking skills.

S: STAND UP

S: SPEAK UP

S: SHUT UP

STAND UP

Fear is actually the adrenalin in a person to be an effective speaker. It is the desire to communicate effectively. Winston Churchill, a remarkable speaker of his times, was once asked by a journalist why he sweated so much on reaching the podium. Was it fear? He retorted: 'This is the sweat of perfection!'

Conquering the fear of public speaking

Public speaking is a common source of stress for many of us. However, it does not have to be stressful.

If you want to overcome the fear of public speaking, you have to keep these key principles in mind.

Key Principles

Speaking in public is not stressful

Public speaking is not stressful. Thousands of human beings have learned to speak in front of groups with little or no stress at all. Many of these people were initially terrified to speak in public. Their knees would shake, their voices would tremble and their thoughts would become jumbled. Yet they learned to overcome their fear of public speaking completely.

If they can conquer the fear of public speaking, so can you! It just takes the right guiding principles, the right understanding and the right plan of action to make this goal a reality.

It's not difficult.

You don't have to be brilliant or perfect to succeed

You don't have to be brilliant, witty or perfect to succeed. That is not what public speaking is all about. You can be average. You can be below average. You can make mistakes, get tongue-tied, or forget whole segments of your talk. You can even tell no jokes at all and still be successful.

It all depends on how you, and your audience, define 'success'. Your audience doesn't expect perfection.

The essence of public speaking is this: give your audience something of value. That's all there is to it. If people in the audience walk away with something or anything of value, they will consider you a success. If they walk away feeling better about themselves, feeling better about some job they have to do, they will consider you a success. If they walk away feeling happy or entertained, they will consider their time with you worthwhile.

Even if you pass out, get tongue-tied or say something stupid during your talk, they won't care! As long as they get something of value, they will be thankful.

They don't even need to feel good to consider you a success. If you criticise people or if you stir them up to ultimately benefit them, they might still appreciate you even though you didn't make them feel good.

All you need is two or three main points

You don't have to deliver heaps of facts or details. While you may choose to include lots of facts and information, you only need to make two or three main points to make your talk successful. You can even have one key point in your whole talk.

You also need a purpose that is right for the task

This principle is very important. One big mistake people make, when they speak in public, is they have the wrong purpose in mind. Often, they have no specific purpose in mind; this causes a whole lot of unnecessary stress and anxiety. This is what is termed as 'hidden cause' of public speaking stress.

You may be good but someone is going to disapprove of either you or your argument. That is just human nature. In a large group of people, there will always be diverse opinions, judgements and reactions. Some will be positive, others will be negative.

The essence of public speaking is to give your audience something of value. The essence here is *give* not *get*! The purpose of public speaking is not for you to get something (approval, fame, respect and clients) from your audience. It is to give something useful to them.

If you focus on giving as much as you can to your audience, you will then be aligned with the essence of public speaking. You will also avoid one of the biggest pitfalls that cause people to experience public speaking anxiety.

The best way to succeed is not to consider yourself a public speaker

The best way to succeed as a public speaker is not to consider yourself as a public speaker at all.

We often assume that to be successful, we must strive very hard to bring forth certain idealistic qualities that we do not possess.

The problem is that we try to become someone other than ourselves. We try to be a public speaker, whatever that image means to us.

The truth about public speaking is that most successful speakers became successful by being themselves. They didn't try to be somebody else. Sincerity and authenticity is the bottom line of public speaking, in fact, in any type of communication. When people are just themselves in front of other people, it is then that they discover how much fun they can have doing something most other people dread.

Don't try to become public speakers! No matter what type of person we are, or what skills and talents we possess, we can stand up in front of others and fully be ourselves. One can be bold, compassionate, silly, informative, helpful, witty or anything one wants. One can tell jokes, humorous or poignant anecdotes, or do anything else that feels natural in the moment.

The speaker is alive; the speaker is geared up. He is fully invested in everything he says and does. That's another gift a speaker can give to his audience. It also allows him to tell when he has gone on too long or when the attention of the people, who are listening to him, begins to stray away.

Sometimes, we enjoy throwing ourselves in front of a group without knowing specifically what we're going to say. The speaker could just focus on the main points and remember that he is there to give people something of value. In many instances, he will say things he's never said before! They just come out of him spontaneously while 'being with his audience'.

Don't try to give talks the way someone else does. Just go out there, armed with a little knowledge and a few key points, and be yourself. Everything else will usually work out.

Humility and humour

Humility and humour can go a long way in making your talks more enjoyable and entertaining for your audience.

If you are comfortable with being humorous, or if it fits your speaking situation, go for it. It usually works, even if you don't do it perfectly.

Humility means standing up in front of others and sharing some of your own human frailties, weaknesses and mistakes. We all have weaknesses; when you stand up in front of others and show that you're not afraid to admit yours, you create a safe, intimate climate where others can acknowledge their personal shortcomings as well.

But beware; don't begin your talk with the cliché: 'I couldn't prepare this talk as I was busy, but I will talk on…' This will be a confession that you are here to waste time.

Being humble in front of others makes you more credible, more believable and paradoxically more respected. People can connect with you more easily. You become 'one of them'. It also sets a tone of honesty and self-acceptance. True humility is easily distinguished from the pretence of acting humble. If you pretend, your audience will perceive this and lose respect for you.

Humour and humility can be combined very effectively. Telling humorous stories about yourself, or using your own personal failings to demonstrate a point that you are trying to make can be both entertaining and illuminating.

If you get nervous when you stand up to speak in front of a group, don't hide this fact from your audience. Be real and humble; acknowledge your fears openly and honestly.

You can start your talk with a humorous story that produces the same effect. Try wit also: 'tough reasonableness'. This is an intellectual quality. Humour has an undercurrent of feeling.

Believe: When you speak in public, nothing 'bad' can ever happen!

What if they all get up and leave after the first ten minutes? What if they put up harsh questions or comments once I'm done? What if someone in the audience tries to turn the group against me?

Most of these things don't happen. Just in case they do, it's useful to have a strategy in mind.

Most of the 'negative' things that happen when one is speaking can be handled by keeping one principle in mind—everything that happens can be used to one's advantage.

If people get up and start to head for the door, I can stop what I'm doing and ask for feedback.

- Was there something about my topic, my style or my manner of presentation that was offensive?
- Were they simply in the wrong room at the start and didn't know it?
- Did someone misinform them about what my talk was going to cover?

Even if everyone walked out and refused to give a reason, one could ultimately find ways to benefit from this experience.

You don't have to control the behaviour of your audience

To succeed as a public speaker, you don't have to control the behaviour of your audience. You do, however, need to control your own thoughts, preparation, arrangement for audio-visual aids, and how the room is laid out. But the one thing you don't have to do is to control your audience.

If people are restless, don't try to control them. If someone is talking to a person next to him, or reading the newspaper, or has fallen asleep, leave them alone. If people look like they aren't paying attention, refrain from criticising them.

In general, the more you prepare, the worse you might do

Preparation is useful for any public appearance.

If you have the wrong focus (i.e. purpose), if you try to do too much, if you want everyone to applaud your every word, if you fear something bad might happen or you might make a minor mistake, then you can create stress for yourself. In this case, the more effort you put in, the worse you will probably do.

Remember, if you know your subject well, or if you've spoken about it many times before, you may only need a few minutes to prepare sufficiently. All you might need is to remind yourself of the two or three key points you want to make.

Over-preparation usually means you don't feel confident about your ability to speak in public. You'll need to develop trust in your natural ability to speak successfully. Solicit opportunities to speak on your subject in public. If you have something of value to tell others, keep getting in front of people and deliver it. In no time at all, you'll gain confidence.

Your audience truly wants you to succeed

The last principle to remember is that your audience truly wants you to succeed. Most of them are scared of public speaking, just like you. They know the risk of embarrassment, humiliation and failure that people take every time they present themselves in public. So they will feel for you. They will admire your courage. The audience will be on your side, no matter what happens.

> **Hidden Causes Of Public Speaking Stress**
> - Thinking that public speaking is stressful, it's not
> - Thinking you need to be brilliant or perfect to succeed, you don't
> - Trying to impart too much information or cover too many points in a short presentation
> - Having the wrong purpose in mind
> - Trying to please everyone (this is unrealistic)
> - Trying to emulate other speakers (difficult) rather than simply being your true self (easy)
> - Failing to be frank and upfront
> - Being fearful of potential negative outcomes
> - Trying to control the wrong things, such as the behaviour of your audience
> - Spending too much time over-preparing (instead of developing confidence and trust in your natural ability to succeed)
> - Thinking your audience will be as critical of your performance as you might be.

Key principles to always keep in mind
- Speaking in public is not stressful.
- You don't have to be brilliant or perfect to succeed.
- All you need is two or three main points.
- You also need a purpose that is right for the task.
- The best way to succeed is not to consider yourself a public speaker.
- Humility and humour can go a long way.
- When you speak in public, nothing 'bad' can ever happen!
- You don't have to control the behaviour of your audience.
- In general, the more you prepare, the worse you might do.
- Your audience truly wants you to succeed.

Dos and don'ts of public speaking

Dos	Don'ts
Prepare your speech	Don't read out your speech or learn your speech
Practice	Don't apologise
Relax	Don't use slides with too much information
Start your speech with a punch-line	Don't fall in love with the sound of your voice

Dos	Don'ts
Say it like you mean it	Don't lean while speaking; maintain eye contact

SPEAK UP

I keep six honest serving men (they taught me all I know). Their names are: 'What', 'Why', 'When', 'How', 'Where' and 'Who'.

WHAT AND WHY

Deciding The Objective

General Objectives	Specific Objectives
To persuade or sell To teach To stimulate thought To inform To entertain*	These depend on the subject matter entirely

*Whatever be your general objective, there is always a need to entertain your audience. This does not mean cracking jokes. It means that the material must be put across in such a way that it is interesting and people want to listen to it.

Note: It is an excellent idea to write down the objective of the speech in one sentence. This has various benefits.

- It clears the speaker's mind right at the start.
- When your notes are complete, you can check that you are meeting your original aim.

WHO

Researching The Audience

Audience is the most important in the whole exercise.

What should you know about audience?
- How many persons are there?
- Why are they there? Are they there of their own free will? Were they sent to listen? Are they paying?
- What is their present knowledge of the subject of the talk?
- Are they likely to have any bias towards or against the subject or the speaker?
- What are their expectations from the talk and the speaker?
- What age, range and sex are they?

The bottom line is 'response-ability'.

WHERE

Preparing The Environment

It is important to consider where the talk is going to take place.

The size of the room must be aligned with the pitch of your voice.

HOW

How Things In The Room Work

Become aware of:
- any likely distractions for you and your audience.
- the possibility of noise/general interruption.

Pitch your speech at the right level: A woman talking to a group of men about women's equality would be different when talking to a group of women. Similarly, a computer expert will talk differently with experts and novices.

WHEN

Timing

- **Time of the day:** After lunch session is known as the 'Graveyard' session in training circles.
- **How long does one get:** Keep to time.
- **Right amount of material for the talk:** If there is no clock in the room, take off your watch and put it on the podium.

SEATING

Theatre Style

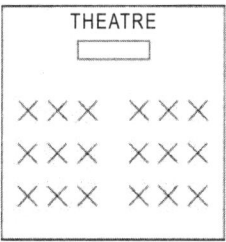

Formal atmosphere and eye contact with the audience is difficult to achieve.

Horse-shoe

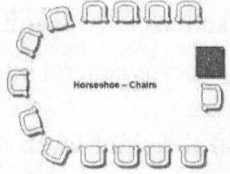

Single row of people seated in a horse-shoe shape is informal and conducive to participation.

Curved

Similar problems as with the theatre style but slightly less formal.

Cabaret Rows

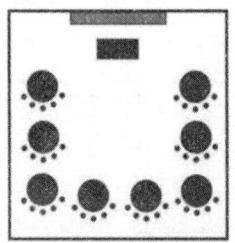

People sitting in groups around tables; it is useful if you break the audience into formal discussion groups.

Points to watch

- Most people have a tendency of having too many chairs. Rope off the back rows.
- Ideally, you want the audience as close to you as possible.
- Try to make sure the seats are not too comfortable. Low, soft chairs can be sleep inducing—the last thing you want from the audience.
- The environment you have can either hinder or help. The aim is to minimise the hindrances and maximise the good points.

Concentration Problems

Concentrating hard for long is often difficult. Concentration level: two hours.

Concentration Curve

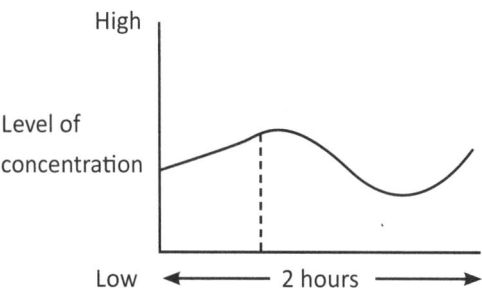

Concentration is good for the first twenty minutes or so. It becomes difficult to concentrate after that.

> **General preparation**
> - Why am I speaking? Clarify objective.
> - Who am I speaking to? Research the audience.
> - Where am I speaking? Familiarise yourself with the venue and equipment. Anticipate distractions. Arrange the seating suitably.
> - When am I speaking? Time of the day? How long have I got? Anticipate lack of concentration.

Preparing The Material

- Any speech will almost certainly fail unless careful thought is given to the subject matter.

These stages will help your thought process in the preparation of the material and ensure that your speech is well structured and lively.

Stage One: Brainstorming

- It is essential to get all thoughts and ideas about your subject down on paper; useful method—make pattern notes.
- Take a plain sheet of paper. Write the objectives of your talk at the top and the main points of your talk in the centre of the page, in a circle.
- Write down all the ideas and thoughts you have on the subject, starting from the circle and branching out along lines of connecting ideas.
- Let your mind be as free as possible. Do not restrict your thoughts by deciding where each point should go in a list. Your ideas should flow easily.

- When finished, circle any related ideas and sections and establish your order of priorities and organisation.

COMPLETED PATTERN NOTE

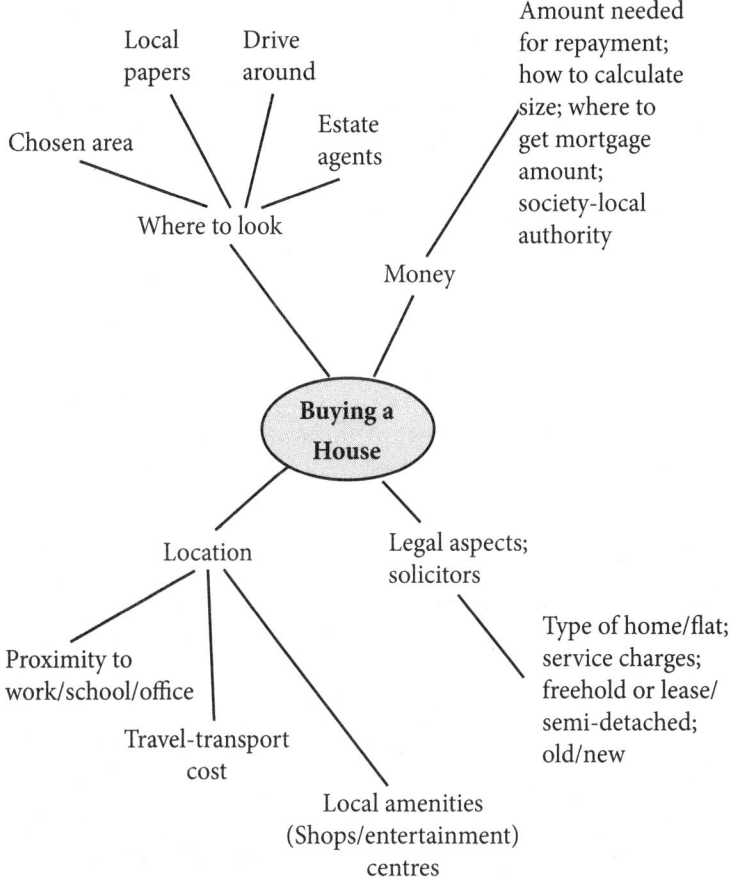

Stage Two: Structuring And Selecting

- Important to keep the number of main points to a minimum.
- In a forty-five-minute speech, you should not try to make more than five main points.
- In a five-minute speech—make one or two main points.
- You should concentrate on and write the 'middle' of the speech first.
  - Objective
  - Audience
  - How long have I got?
  - Use 'must' 'should', and 'could,' based on who the audience is.
    - Must—How it will operate?
    - Should—Why the decision to install?
    - Could—Why this system has been chosen against any other?

Stage Three: Illustrating

- As a speaker—talk in pictures; create mental images.

Stage Four: Opening

Introduction: The introduction can look like this.

> Interest: Find something to capture the attention of the audience immediately. Preferably not the usual lines like 'Unaccustomed as I am to public speaking…'

> **N**eed: Show the audience why they need to listen.
>
> **T**itle and **R**ange: Tell them the subject of your talk and what you are going to cover.
>
> **O**bjective: Objective should be clear to your audience.

INTRO: Interest Need Title Range Objective

Closing:

- Should be conclusive. It should not just drift to a halt with words like 'I think that's all I've got to say…'
- Remember that what you say in the end is the thought you leave your audience with.
- Summarise your main points again.

Note: It is essential to write your opening and closing sentences in full and incorporate them into your notes. The opening sentence will help you to get started and when you have spoken, the closing lines will let you know that you have come to the end.

Stage Five: Notes

- Notes should be brief and comprise keywords.
- Those who use verbatim notes are really reading out aloud rather than speaking from within. Also, completely written out speeches sound stilted even if learned by heart. This is because written English and spoken English are not the same.

- If you are making a particularly important speech, it is an excellent idea to write the whole thing out in full, practice and then reduce it all to key notes—so that you are able to look at the audience rather than at your notes.

Notes are best put on cards. There are several reasons for this.

- Cards would not shake as much as sheets of paper, if you become nervous.
- You do not need a lectern as cards can be held quite easily.
- Since cards are smaller, they encourage you to use key words rather than writing complete sentences.

Checklist: Preparing the material

- Brainstorm the subject—make pattern notes.
- Structure and Select—keep the main points down to an appropriate number.
- Select on the basis of objective, time, audience, and 'must, should and could'.
- Tell it like news—what you are going to say.

Use Illustrations

- Simplify difficult or complex information. Use real-life examples to illustrate points.

Opening And Closing

- Write opening and closing sentence in full.

- Capture the attention of the audience in the beginning.
- Be conclusive when you have finished your talk.
- Notes—write on cards; use keywords; write timings and pointers for yourself on the cards; clip them together.

Putting Yourself Across

Three 'V's
Verbal—words
Vocal—to do with voice
Visual—facial expressions, gestures and posture

Graded Priority of the three 'V's
Verbal—7 per cent—words
Vocal—38 per cent—tone of voice
Visual—55 per cent—facial expression gesture and posture

Words

- Use simple language. Do not use five words when one would do. For example: Instead of 'in the fullness of time', use 'soon' or 'now'.
- Be conscious of using positive words. Avoid words like 'but', 'try' and 'maybe' etc.
- Talk in sentences and beware of different levels of abstractions.

> **Gauri—the cow**
> Wealth
> Farm asset
> Cow (Keep towards the lower level of the Gauri ladder)

How We Say It

- Expression—emphasise particular words.
- Pausing—do not be afraid of pausing.
- Tone of voice and pitch—a speech delivered in a monotonous tone can sound tedious.
- A voice that moves up and down like a piano scale.
- Speak clearly—be careful of tongue twisting words.

Speak Out

Be loud enough to be heard across the room. Breathing properly can help here. If you do not put enough air into your lungs, you get a rather squeaky voice. Body language—look at the audience and smile—audience smiles back; avoid creating barriers; stand with your feet slightly apart; avoid leaning and keep hands out of pockets.

Problems to be beware of while brainstorming:

- May end up with too much information
- You may leave yourself with a lot of editing work
- Risk of losing focus
- You may end up with unrelated points

Tips For Correct Speaking

When you speak, remember there are two aspects:
- what you say; and
- how you say it.

'*I need your help*' says your boss walking up to your desk. Is it an *order*, a *command*, a *request*, or a *compliment*?

Conversation is partly self-expression. It provides us opportunities for asserting our individuality, telling the world how we feel.

At its best, conversation means pooling information, sharing interests and bringing together ideas.

Speech Is A Form Of Self-Portrait

Speech making falls into two categories: personal and technical. For this, we need a good vocabulary.

GRAMMAR

- *Syntax and accidence:* Instead of 'family members', say 'members of a family'
- *Usage:* Look at roots, branches and fruits of words. (Enthusiasm: En = within + theos (god) = power to create—the Brahma aspect
- *Words:* Distinction and misapplication
- *Balance vocabulary:* Catchphrase; jargon—price-wise, client-wise
- *Voice:* It is the thought behind the words which gives them power, not superficial oratory. So your aim at the start is to be true to yourself. You must endeavour to

reveal your true personality when you speak, suiting your voice with appropriate vocabulary and getting an individual angle on the subject.

- **Stance:** Stand upright; legs slightly apart; hands across the chest; palms downwards and fingertips touching; elbows slightly below the shoulder line.
- **Clarity of diction:** Every word must be enunciated according to its importance, some with more emphasis than others, but all must be heard.
- **Tone and pitch:** We all possess a natural middle tone. Some of us have high-pitched voices than others with different middle registers, so do not try and change this.
- **Timing:** Here, timing is not about our speech length in minutes but how you deliver the material. It involves giving pauses and correct emphasis.
- **'U-m-m's and 'E-r-r's:** Be careful of unnecessary 'u-m-m's and 'e-r-r's.
- **Material and forms of speech making:** Never read out a speech. Train your mind to absorb the content. Memory is a matter of paying attention; it is in itself a filling system. Harvest all material you can.
- **Time:** Keep to your allotted time. Don't get carried away. Always leave your audience wanting more but never give it to them.
- **Meiosis:** This is a disease like name dropping: speaking of a car accident after dinner, describing Miss Right and not the accident.
- **Speech and structure:** Like a short story, it must have a beginning, middle and an end.

Sentences Vary

Loose: My name is Bond.

Periodic: Bond is my name.

Balance: Many tried; few were successful.

Seven ways to be a good conversationalist
- Be interesting
- Be friendly
- Be cheerful
- Be animated, yet relaxed
- Be flexible
- Be tactful
- Be courteous

Eight Don'ts of a conversation
- Don't be dogmatic
- Don't be condescending
- Don't be argumentative
- Don't be lifeless
- Don't be insincere
- Don't be egocentric

Seven flaws in a conversation

- Pet words: fabulous, tremendous
- Superfluous words and phrases: naturally, actually and literally etc.
- Fad words: overall picture, contact and dynamic etc.
- Too much slang: yo, yup and guys etc.
- Affectations: too many foreign words—bête noire, à la carte
- Exaggerating: The funniest story I've ever heard...
- Relating personal experiences awkwardly

Five ways to say 'No'

- Put it on an impersonal basis
- Make it clear that you would like to say 'Yes'
- Say 'No' by helping the person say 'No' to himself
- In saying 'No', show what needs to be done to get a 'Yes'
- Most important, say 'No' in the nicest, warmest way you can

PRESENTATION (EVALUATION)

Name: ....

Posture and stance: ....

Clarity and diction: ....

Audibility: ....

Tone and pitch: ....

Eye contact: ....

Facial expressions: ....

Body language: ....

Gestures: ....

Presentation: ....

Three 'V' Assessment

Verbal: ....

Visual: ....

Other remarks: ....

Introducing a speaker: TIS

T   first, reveal the *topic*.

I   secondly, the *importance* of the subject.

S   finally, say a few words about the *speaker*.

Note: While introducing the speaker, don't turn away from the microphone to reveal his/her name. The name matters the most.

These are the basics of introducing a speaker.

- To dispose the audience favourably towards the speaker
- To underline the importance or relevance of the topic
- To indicate the credentials and competence of the speaker
- Familiarise yourself with the speaker's background; do not read from his biodata unless absolutely necessary; pronounce his/her name correctly
- Be cheerful, warm and enthusiastic; this is contagious
- Avoid the commonplace—'for having graced this occasion by taking time out of his busy schedule'
- Be accurate; don't have the speaker wondering who is being introduced
- Often it is effective to single out one quality or accomplishment of the speaker rather than give an undifferentiated litany of his or her past. Sometimes the method of 'passing over' is helpful.

Give A Vote Of Thanks

A vote of thanks should be like a punctuation mark at the end of a sentence: a full stop, a question mark or an exclamation mark. The average speech calls only for a full stop; a scintillating one for an exclamation mark; while a controversial or tendentious talk may require a question mark. In every case, however, the vote of thanks should be brief.

Here are a few tips for getting the vote of thanks right.

- Be relevant
- Refer to the central thought or position that struck you the most
- Be positive
- This is no time for nitpicking or a display of your analytical skills; emphasise the positive and forget about the negative
- Most speakers go beyond their time; the audience is frequently tired—be brief and gone.

A vote of thanks, then, should add something, i.e. make a positive contribution to the occasion. One of the best vote of thanks that one can expect consists often words: 'Mr Mehra, for the best evening we've had in ages, thank you.'

Five Canons Of Persuasive Presentations

It may be a new process, product or project that the school, industry or organisation should embrace, you should be able to put across a proposal effectively within a limited period of time.

Purpose

Be absolutely clear about your purpose. You should be able to state in one clear sentence what you wish to accomplish.

The objective of your presentation may not be the same as the objective of your proposal.

Preparation

- Research your audience (individuals or organisation) thoroughly. What problems or needs do they have related to your proposal? Who are the decision-makers? How open minded are they likely to be?
- Know exactly how much time you will be given: allocate it for input, audio-visuals, questions and answers.
- See the room where you will make the presentation. Where will you stand? Will you need a microphone?
- Have your equipment ready to run—charts, transparencies and slides checked for proper order; projector, tape recorder and LCD at the desired volume and focus, needing only a 'switch on' to run.

Problem

Your introduction needs to grab the audience's attention. It must answer the question: 'Why should I listen?'

Make your listeners identify with you through your knowledge of their situation and needs. Show the gap between 'what is' and 'what could be'. Have a clear structure for your message and repeat it; how you organise your remarks largely determines how much of your message will be retained.

Possibilities

Identify and evaluate the different ways of closing the gap between actual and ideal.

Proposal

With enthusiasm, show how your proposal meets their needs better than any other possibility. Handle questions pleasantly. Close exactly on time.

PERFECT SPEAKER

- A good speaker is lively, interested, enthusiastic and vital. He is interested in his topic, so he speaks about it with enthusiasm.

- A good speaker is earnest. He doesn't talk for sake of it, to show off his clothes, smile, diction or voice. He doesn't turn on the charm when he stands up only to switch it off as he sits down.

- A good speaker has a sense of responsibility to his listeners. He realises that if he talks for five minutes to a hundred listeners, he is taking five hundred minutes out of their lives. He tries to say something that will be worthy of their time.

- If he has been allotted been five minutes, he does not take ten. He takes care not to squeeze others off the programme, or force them to hurry. They, too, may have something worthwhile to say.

- A good speaker has a sense of responsibility to his subject. He doesn't bite off more than he can chew. He doesn't spread it thin.

- He has a sense of leadership. He stands tall, speaks responsibly and with authority, as a leader should. He is positive, friendly and straight-forward.
- A good speaker keeps his head. He doesn't get carried away by enthusiasm. He doesn't let his confidence become overconfidence. He doesn't let himself get intoxicated from the sense of power that comes from being in the public eye.
- A good speaker tries to be balanced.
- A good speaker keeps his sense of humour.
- He says what he thinks and not what some columnist or newscaster thinks.
- He studies other speakers, but doesn't imitate them.
- He recognises and admires the fine qualities he has. He works out his own style and discovers what will make him an effective speaker. He knows himself.
- He does not indulge in wishful thinking about his speaking abilities. He is realistic.
- A good speaker learns to accept criticism.
- He is aware of his weaknesses and doesn't cover them up. He does something to correct them.

Be aware of your strengths. Emphasise them and develop them.

IMPROMPTU SPEAKING

There are times when we are asked to get up and say a few words about someone or a topic when we have not planned on saying anything at all. We are more shocked than anyone else. Has this ever happened to you? If and when this does happen to you, be prepared to rise to the challenge.

Here are a few tips.

- Decide quickly what your message will be—Keep in mind that you have not been asked to give a speech but to make some impromptu remarks. Pick one message, comment and focus on that one central idea. Many times, other ideas may come to you after you start speaking.
- Do not try and memorise what you will say—Trying to memorise will only make you more nervous and you will find yourself thinking more about the words and not about the message.
- Start off strong and with confidence—If you at least plan your opening statement, this will get you started on the right foot. Getting started is the most difficult. Plan what your first sentence will be. If you know you have three points or ideas to talk about, just start off simply by saying, 'I would just like to talk about three points'.

  The first point is...the second point is...and so on. This keeps you within your desired ambit.
- Decide on your transitions from one point to the next—After you have decided on your opening remark or line, come up with a simple transition statement that takes you to your main point. If you have more than one point to make, you can use a natural transition such as, 'My second point is…' or 'My next point is...' Just list your points. Do not write the exact words, but just the points you want to mention.

- Maintain eye contact with the audience—This is easier to do if you do not have a written script. Maintain eye contact with your audience and speak from your heart. Focus on communicating to your audience and not speaking at them.
- Occasionally, throw in an off-the-cuff remark because you want your style to be flexible and seem impromptu; trust your instinct and add a few words which just pop into your head. Keep it conversational and think of the audience as a group of your friends.
- Finally, have a good conclusion—'And the last point I would like to make is ...' Once you have made your last point, you can then turn back to the person who asked you to speak in the first place.

With a little practice, this process will feel more natural to you. Anticipating that you may be asked to say a few words should force you to at least think about what you might say if you are asked to speak. Then if you are asked, you are better prepared because you anticipated being asked.

Gestures

Gestures are reflections of every speaker's individual personality. What's right for one speaker may not be right for another. These rules apply to anyone who seeks to become a dynamic, effective speaker.

- **Respond naturally to what you think, feel and see:** It's natural for you to gesture, and it's unnatural for you not to. If you inhibit your impulse to gesture, you will probably become tense.

- **Create the condition for gesturing, not the gesture:** When you speak, you should be totally involved in communicating—not thinking about your hands. Your gestures should be motivated by the content of your presentation.
- **Suit the action to the word and the occasion:** Your visual and verbal messages must function as partners in communicating the same thought or feeling. Every gesture you make should be purposeful and reflective of your words so the audience will note only the effect, not the gesture itself. Don't overdo the gesturing; you'll divert the listener's attention away from your message. Young audience is usually attracted to a speaker who uses vigorous gestures, but older and more conservative groups may feel irritated or threatened by a speaker whose physical actions are overwhelming.
- **Make your gestures convincing:** Your gestures should be lively and distinct if they are to convey the intended impressions. Effective gestures are vigorous enough to be convincing yet slow enough to be clearly visible without being overpowering.
- **Make your gestures smooth and well timed:** Every gesture has three parts:
  - The approach—your body begins to move in anticipation;
  - The stroke—the gesture itself; and
  - The return—this brings your body back to a balanced posture.

The flow of a gesture—the approach, the stroke, the return—must be smoothly executed so that only the stroke is evident to the audience. While it is advisable to practise gesturing, don't try to memorise your every move. This makes your gesturing stilted and ineffective.

- **Make natural, spontaneous gesturing a habit:** The first step in becoming adept at gesturing is to determine what you are doing.

  To improve gestures, practice—but never during a speech. Practise gesturing while speaking informally to friends, members of the family and co-workers.

USING LCD PROJECTORS

Read The LCD Projector Manual

Not all LCD projectors work the same way and each has its own unique operating requirements. Familiarise yourself with the projector before using it during the presentation. Make sure your computer can be properly interfaced with the LCD projector.

Practise Setting Up The Equipment Several Times

Spend some time making sure you know how to properly set up the LCD projector with your computer and other computers. Set up the LCD projector in the actual presentation environment you will be using, if possible.

Set Up The Equipment Well In Advance

Allow yourself plenty of time to set up your computer and the LCD projector. Check any last-minute details.

Check The Bulb's Life

LCD projector bulbs have a limited life. Some bulbs have shorter lives than others. Check to make sure the bulb you will be using is not close to the end of its life.

Bring Spare Bulbs And Cables

Always carry spare bulbs with you and make sure you know how to properly change the bulb. Also, remember, 'Hot' glass looks like 'Cold' glass; be careful and bring a towel or glove to use when changing the bulb. Practise changing the bulb during one of your practice sessions.

Check Your Presentation For Colour Combinations

Take some time to check out the presentation for the colour combinations you will be using. Some colours and colour combinations do not project well.

Check The Font Size You Are Using

Nothing is more frustrating to an audience than text that cannot be easily seen or read. Make sure you are using the proper text size for the distance you will be projecting your slides.

Many presentations, today, are followed by a question-and-answer session. For some people, this can be the most exciting part of the presentation. For others, it can be their worst nightmare. In fact, there are some presenters who avoid the question-and-answer session altogether.

Handling Questions: Five Steps

- Too many people start responding to a question before the entire question has even been asked. Not waiting to hear the entire question can result in you providing a response which has nothing to do with the question. Force yourself to listen to the entire question and make sure you understand it.

- Pause and allow yourself time to value the question and the listener. Repeat the question out loud so that the entire audience can hear it. It is important that everyone hears the question or the answer that you provide may not make sense to some of them. Repeating the question, will allow you some additional time to evaluate the question and formulate a response.

- Credit the person for asking the question. You may say something like, 'That was a great question' or 'Glad you asked that question'. A word of caution: If you credit one person with asking a question, be sure to credit everyone who asks a question. You don't want some people to feel that their question was not as important as others.

- Respond to the question honestly and as best as you can. If you do not know the answer to a question, do not try to fake it. Be honest and tell them you do not know the answer, but do promise to research it for them and do get back to them.

- Bridge the gap to the next question by asking a

question. 'Does that answer your question?', 'Is that the kind of information you were looking for?' This is critical. Once they respond to you, with a 'Yes', you can go on to the next person. This also gives them an opportunity to say 'No' and further clarify their question by asking it again.

Handling Questions: Additional Tips

- Ask people to stand up when they ask a question. This does two things. First, you are able to see who is asking the question. Second, it also makes it easier for the audience to hear the question.
- Provide small sheets of paper for people to write down their questions during your presentation, lest they may forget what they were going to ask by the time the question-and-answer session starts.
- Allow people to pass the questions to you, if they feel uncomfortable standing up and asking the question out loud. This gives an option to the person who truly wants to ask a question.
- Always repeat the question. This does three things. First, it ensures that you have understood the question. Second, it gives you a chance to value the question and think of an answer. Third, it ensures that everyone in the audience can hear the question since you are facing them.
- Always think 'before' you answer a question. This allows you time to think, especially for difficult questions. Do the same to questions you readily know the answers for. Responding too quickly to questions

you are most comfortable with, will only draw attention to the questions you are not too comfortable with.

- Write down the questions you couldn't answer. This way, you can properly follow-up with the person who asked the question that you couldn't answer. Be sure to get their name and phone number or address. Promise to get back to them and do get back to them.

Keynote Address

A keynote address is aimed at presenting the issues of primary interest to an assembly and often to generate enthusiasm.

- **Don't try to fool:** It probably won't work. Audiences are very perceptive. They know when the speaker is focused and 'walks the talk'. They also know when the presenter is just giving a book report, having spent a little time in preparation to learn about the high points of the topic presented. When you are the keynoter, you have to be a fountainhead of knowledge.

- **Don't read the text:** We liked hearing stories read to us as children. But our audiences are adults. They want to experience what is in your heart and in your mind. Notes to guide you through the important points are fine, but if you are reading text, you may as well hire a professional actor who is trained to bring a script to life. As your audience reacts to a particular point, expand on it. Feed them what they need most.

- **Don't use inside stories:** Be sure to mention events or anecdotes about something that most of your audience will know nothing about. Isolate the majority of your audience. Keep them in the dark. Make them feel that they are not among the chosen few. Use the time to have a private, inside dialogue with someone.

- **Don't crack jokes on your audience:** Humour is a wonderful communication tool (if you are witty). Self-deprecating humour reveals your own vulnerabilities. Stories about people and events, other than your audience, if in good taste, will set the tone for a positive learning environment. But if you direct your humour directly at your audience, you set up an 'us versus him/her' climate that will interfere with your message getting across. Attacking an audience, even if not meant to offend, will tend to make them defensive and distrustful of the speaker.
- **Don't go over the time limit:** You have a contract with your audience. Their obligation is to be attentive. Yours is to deliver the material promised and to do it within the allocated time frame. If you are given twenty minutes, finish in twenty minutes.

  If no time frame is announced, tell the audience up front how much of their time will you take. ('We are going to be together for the next forty-five minutes and during this time...').

Conference Speaking: Stand Up

- Being invited to speak at a conference is a nice experience.
- Preparing your speech focuses your mind on the important topics you will talk about, and helps you

marshal and organise your thoughts on your area of expertise.
- Have a specified amount of time to speak and think how best to communicate.
- Nothing speeds up your heart beat like public speaking, and most of us could do with some practice.
- Engaging with other speakers helps improve your performance.
- It helps cement your reputation as an expert in your field.

TIPS FOR A GOOD CONFERENCE PRESENTATION: ACADEMIC AND BUSINESS

Follow Convention

People attend conferences to be briefed on topics which they need to know about. They have busy lives and want to leave the conference knowing something new. They want to hear an expert talk about their area of expertise—calmly, authoritatively and factually. The main rule of public speaking is: stand up, speak up and shut up. Be interesting, be clever and be engaging, but if the organiser asks for twenty minutes on the future of 'peer pressure and cyber pressure', it's because that's what he has told the delegates they will get and it's what the delegates have paid their fee for. Some speakers try to be funny, unconventional or quirky, and it usually doesn't work. Keep it simple, follow the rules and give the audience what they demand.

Remember: KISS—**K**eep **I**t **S**hort and **S**imple.

Agree To The Terms Of Reference

Usually, a conference organiser will invite you to speak on a general topic and you'll mutually agree to the points you'll cover. If you commit to covering those points, then cover them.

Speaking Alongside A Famous Person

Conference organisers like to invite a famous person to give a keynote speech because it's a good hook to get people to attend their event. You might be lucky—you may be the famous person; if so, well done. But it's more likely that you'll be on the agenda alongside a government minister, an international expert or a media celebrity. Think carefully if you're scheduled to speak before or after the 'star.' While you may be able to bask in reflected glory, they do have a tendency to overshadow other speakers and possibly the event as a whole. Some speakers lose the attention of their audience when a celebrity arrives in the middle of their speech and all eyes turn away from the speaker and towards that person.

Assert Yourself

You've been invited to speak at a conference because someone thinks you've something interesting to say, which the delegates should hear. You've got to explain to them what your opinion on the topic is—the one they should pay attention to. Outline briefly and the audience will pay attention. Plan your speech to tell them something they didn't know or wouldn't know by reading research papers.

Flexibility

Do ask the organiser for a delegate list. Get a general idea of who is attending the conference and what their expectations are, and fit your presentation to that. You need to go to the audience; they won't come to you. An academic audience has very different expectations from a business audience; you should be careful to give the right speech to the right crowd. You should also fit your speech to the time of day—in general, speeches in the morning are more formal than speeches in the afternoon when the delegates have had a chance to mingle, chat and relax. If you're speaking immediately after lunch, then you've got to try twice as hard to get their attention because they'll be sleepy. If you're the last speaker of the day, then it's likely that the conference will be running late and the audience will be thinking about going home. Don't delay them or you'll be the person they blame for getting home late. These are important issues to take into account when preparing your speech.

Listen To Previous Speakers

You must at least listen to a couple of speakers before you, so you can assess the mood of the event. Each conference has its own atmosphere and a good speaker will be able to read that atmosphere and adapt their speech to fit it. Some conferences are serious and the audience will sit in silence and not ask any questions; others are more interactive and you should be able to cope with both. Speakers who fail to read the audience give a totally inappropriate speech.

People Can't Read And Listen At The Same Time

If you use PowerPoint and have a slide showing a complex graph, give the audience a couple of seconds to decode it before you start talking. If the audience is reading your slide, they're not listening to you. If they've been given a printout of the presentation, it's likely they're reading it and not listening. It's also likely they've turned to the last page and are mentally counting the seconds until you reach the last slide.

Remember that people are doing this. Remember the rule: show, don't tell. If you begin your presentation by telling people you wish to discuss the four main trends in business sector, then your audience will expect to be told what they are, and be reminded which of the four topics you're discussing at any given moment.

Ask the conference organiser if delegates will be emailed a copy of the PowerPoint presentation or if it will be put online. If not, tell the audience you'll email it to them. This means they don't have to write down everything for the fear of missing something. They can put down their pens, sit back and listen to you. It makes for a better presentation.

Keep It Simple

In a thirty-minute presentation (the maximum time you're likely to be given), you're not going to say everything you want, so break up your message into three or four important topics. If a topic doesn't naturally fit into your overall message, leave it out and concentrate on your core issues. Look at the audience and get their feedback. Are they confused? Are they taking it in? Do they need a break? Are they bored? Do they need more background information? Can you skip a section? Can you leave out some of the background information and go straight to the heart of the presentation? If you're not sure what their body language is telling you, ask them. Assert and reassert your main points throughout your speech.

Take Time To Summarise

At the end of your talk, wrap it up. Don't just finish with an abrupt 'thank you' and scuttle off the stage. Take a moment to summarise your thoughts and reassert your message.

If you are running out of time, don't skip the summary. Skip an earlier part instead.

Find Out If You Need To Take Questions

The conference organiser will have told you if you'll be answering questions or if there'll be a panel discussion after your speech. A good tip if you're taking questions is to repeat the question you're asked—not everyone in the audience will have heard what the question was, even if there are microphones, and the experience of repeating the question will help you gather your thoughts. Respond to the question and if you think your answer is too long, invite the questioner to contact you later and discuss it over coffee or after the conference is over.

Make Sure To Leave Your Contact Details

If you're using PowerPoint, make sure your email address is clearly shown on your presentation. Many people will contact you and ask a question they were too nervous to ask on that day, or which only occurred to them when they got home. Even though the speech is over, you're still available on call.

Stand up, speak up, shut up

USING CUE CARDS

The three presentation styles:
- Memorise the presentation
- Write a full script and read from it
- Cue cards—keep short notes by using planning cards

If you memorise, you:
- waste time and effort.
- have to concentrate—the style can become stilted.

Reading from a fully scripted presentation invariably leads to a dull and boring monologue. It is also likely to reduce eye contact and general spontaneity with a resultant loss of impact.

These problems can generally only be overcome by employing a professional speech writer to write the presentation and a professional actor to deliver it.

The use of natural conversational language assisted by pre-prepared cues is almost always the best style for a business presentation. It will help you to sound normal, natural and spontaneous. It will also create a less formal and more relaxed relationship between you and your audience.

Using Planning Cards

Placing the facts and information, that you have collated, in the correct place within your presentation (structure) is a critical process. Speech-aided cue cards are one of the best ways to put the facts into their effective sequence to support your ideas. Write each fact and piece of information on a separate planning card—these are typically the size of a small postcard. Then by shuffling the sequence of points around, you will be able to experiment until you find the right sequence of points that will have the best effect.

During this process, you may decide to make alterations to your original structure, changing the sequence and relationship between certain messages. Remember that it is the impact and clarity of the messages that is important and not sticking rigidly to a structure that can be improved.

You may also find that certain facts and information are more effective in supporting an alternative message to the one which you had originally envisaged—if that is the case, move the facts. Remember that the rule of thumb when screening your research information is to stop adding facts when your point is clear and present them in order of importance.

Using Cue Cards

At this time, you should have a clear picture of your presentation. You will know the overall message—that is, the aim statement. You will have devised a series of key points and the messages and sub-messages—organised in order of importance, the facts and information that you are going to use—and these will be clearly numbered. Convert your planning cards to cue cards.

These are common presentation aids and their role is precisely to give a cue to the presenter.

This example shows how the information on a fact card might be converted to a cue card.

- The best public speakers take time to learn about their audience so that what they're saying is what the audience is interested in hearing.
- The best public speakers know that timing is everything. They find out exactly what their allotted speaking time is and then practice getting their timing right so they don't over-run or under-run.
- The best public speakers appreciate the value of time-out. They leave a 'cushion' of time before and after they speak, to reduce stage fright.
- On an average, you'll want to practise your presentation aloud at least three times to work on your opening and closing, your non-verbal language and your voice intonation.
- The best public speakers are aware that time marches on. While the first thirty-sixty seconds of a presentation seem like hours due to an elevated stress level, the stress subsides as you proceed with your purpose and realise that the audience is there because they need what you have to offer.

Finally, there's no time like the present to work on your public speaking. Every time you speak, it's a form of public speaking.

Remember: Stand up, speak up and shut up.

Writing Skills

When we think of writing, the image of a person sitting at his desk with sheets of paper before him, a pen in his hand and an inkwell on the table rarely comes to mind. But that was how writers practiced their craft in the olden days. In those days, the only tools a writer needed were an imaginative and creative mind, a powerful vocabulary, a flair and passion for writing, a pen, and a few sheets of paper.

Quill was the writing instrument that dominated the early years of writing for more than 1,400 years. Later, the quill was replaced by the fountain pen. Lewis Waterman invented the fountain pen and got a patent for it in 1884. With the invention of fountain pens, writers could spend more time thinking and writing rather than preparing their writing instruments and ink. The ballpoint pen made its appearance in 1938; it was invented by Laszlo Biro, a journalist from Hungary. Writing instruments continued to evolve and got better, thus making writing less cumbersome.

Writers inspire, motivate, inform, engage, excite, empower and take their readers through a range of emotions from absolute bliss to utter dismay—wars start and end, treaties and pacts get signed, people become famous or notorious, heroes are praised and villains punished, courtships start, love blooms and blossoms, lovers get married, some marriages end in divorces, people gossip and spy on each other, and countries flourish and perish—all at the stroke of a pen.

Prophet Muhammad (Peace Be Upon Him) is quoted as saying 'The ink of the scholar's pen is holier than the blood of the martyr.'

In 1839, English author Edward Bulwer-Lytton coined the adage 'The pen is mightier than the sword.' This is undoubtedly true!

The power of words cannot be over-emphasised. According to Lord Byron: 'Words are things; and a small drop of ink, falling like dew upon a thought, produces that which makes thousands, perhaps millions think.'

Writers should master words and learn everything that will make their writing more accurate, effective, captivating, attractive and influential.

Modern writers need all skills their predecessors possessed. The skills remain the same—an imaginative and creative mind, powerful vocabulary, and a flair and passion for writing—but the tools have changed. The quill was replaced by pen, which is being replaced by computers.

It is true: once a new technology rolls out, if you are not part of the steamroller, you are not part of the road. This is true in the case of computers and Information Technology (IT). In today's information age, knowledge of computers is a must. We use computers, either directly or indirectly, in each and every aspect of our lives. Computers, the Internet and IT are changing the way writers write, copyeditors edit, reviewers review and readers read.

Today, an author can publish what he has written in a matter of seconds. He can upload it on his blog, which will be read by people all over the world who can comment about the article, recommend it to friends, and so on. All this can happen in a matter of minutes. Writers can work from anywhere in the world and their audience is the entire world. The canvas is immense; the dimensions are varied.

EVERY WORD COUNTS

Vigorous writing is concise. A sentence should contain no unnecessary words, a paragraph no unnecessary sentences, for the same reason that a drawing should have no unnecessary lines and a machine no unnecessary parts. This does not mean that the writer makes all the sentences short or that he avoids detail and treats his subject only in outline.

Writing is a talent that is not difficult to develop; it needs time, patience and special techniques to master. One can enhance this skill by continuously writing as practice can do it all. Whether writing a blog or a business letter, an email or an essay, the primary goal should be to cater directly and evidently to the requirements and interests of the audience one is addressing.

Writing can be of many types—creative writing, academic writing, professional copywriting, and the list goes on. But the basics are the same for all kinds and types of writing. If you get them right, then nothing can stop you from being a good writer. These skills can help you to enhance your writing skills as it is important to have a command over the language as well as editing techniques. Writing alone does not do it all. What is more important is to develop the skill to rewrite.

MULTUM IN PARVO: MUCH IN LESS

You can write, but can you write well? A good writer is like a sculptor. He uses fewer words to express more. A sculptor takes a mound of clay as the medium and reduces it to give it form and beauty. Similarly, a good writer edits useless words and makes every word count. The canon in writing is '*multum in parvo*' meaning 'much in less'. 'Only the hand that erases can write the true thing.'

Remember: Correct sentences are written; good sentences are often rewritten.

> **Dos** and **Don'ts** for effective writing
> - Be simple
> - Have clarity
> - Remember: Brevity is the soul of wit
> - Let us use our words the way we spend our money
> - Learning to write is learning to think
>   - Try to use picture words rather than abstract words. For example, use 'bus', 'car' or 'train' in place of 'vehicle', and 'cat' or 'dog' in place of 'animal'.
>   - Write less; say more. Use one-syllable words rather than two-syllable words, two-syllable words rather than three etc., for example, use 'blood, tears, sweat and toil', in place of 'sacrifice, sorrow, perspiration and effort' and 'subsequently' in place of 'later'. Not more than 25 per cent of your words should have more than two syllables. Prefer vivid picture words to abstract words.

- Write as you talk. Use active voice rather than passive. For example, say 'I fixed the bicycle' instead of 'The bicycle was fixed by me'.
- Use 'verbs'. They are words that denote action. Choose strong graphic verbs, for instance, 'Shahrukh struggled with the problem for days.' If you choose an effective verb, then an adverb is not needed.
- Each word counts. Don't use two words where one can do the needful.
- Ideally, sentences should not exceed eighteen words. Keep clauses short. Eighteen is the danger alarm!
- One paragraph should talk about one idea. Clear writing comes from clear thinking. You don't know anything clearly, unless you can state it in writing.
- Relate to the experience of your audience, for instance, if you are writing for computer buffs, then you should include terms such as hardware, software, data entry, input and output etc.
- Write not to **impress** but to **express**.
- The reader loses interest quickly. To hold his/her interest, be as personal as the situation allows. Use pronouns (I, you and she etc.) and ask questions. Urge the reader to be with you and even read between the lines.
- Writing is hard work: exert yourself. 'I think, therefore, I am,' said René Descartes. Indeed, writing is a form of therapy.

> **Remember:** Good sentences are not written, they are simply rewritten. Words move; music moves. Every language has its own music. Read your work aloud to see whether it has the correct 'feel'. Sound comes before meaning as we know from our kindergarten days.

Rules for Brevity in Writing

- It is what you make of a story, not the story itself.
- Never summarise without reason.
- Conduct an enquiry.
- Use your experiences.
- Develop your own voice.
- Offer a point of view.
- Think about the craft: Is the writing too loose or has the document been written without sufficient concentration?
- Consider the 'critical thinking' rubric.

Importance Of Brevity

The purpose of writing is to communicate a particular message. It is harder to be brief with a message than it is to write a lengthy piece. This is because we tend to communicate all of our ideas at one go. The point of brevity is not just to say less, but also to communicate a message more concisely. By editing and deleting redundant words or sentences, this is possible.

> Important questions to answer:
> - Can it be made better?
> - Can I make it clearer?
> - What details can I leave out?
> - Can I restructure the sentences?

Trim The Matter—Remove The Unnecessary Load

The tighter the message, the easier it is for readers to grasp it. So, it is important to make each word tell part of the story.

Eliminate Words

Avoid superfluous nouns, verbs, articles, prepositions that obscure meaning rather than clarify it. Avoid 'the fact that,' 'who is' and 'which was'. These are the most commonly used redundant words. Here are a few more examples.

- 'the field of technology' and 'the technology industry' become 'technology'
- 'the volume of total sales increased' becomes 'sales increased'
- 'have a tendency to' becomes 'tend to'
- 'are going to' becomes 'will'
- 'some of the people' becomes 'some people'
- 'I am writing in regard to' becomes 'I'm writing about'

Choose Your Words Carefully

Choose concrete, precise terms

- 'organisation' becomes 'group'
- 'utilise' or 'utilisation' becomes 'use'
- 'morbidity' or 'mortality' becomes 'illness' or 'death'
- 'interface with each other' becomes 'collaborate'

Use Active Voice

Using 'active voice' helps to make every word tell part of the story as compared to 'passive voice', which is more verbose and less dynamic.

'The class was taught by me' becomes 'I taught the class'

'There's a lot of support for the proposition' becomes 'Many people support the proposition'.

Write First, Edit Later

Don't worry about writing concisely the first time. First write, and then make edits. In your first read, you will notice words or sentences that are redundant or don't make sense. Then read again and make more edits. Brevity is important, but so is clarity. If your piece is brief but not clear, then the purpose is defeated. When you get the brevity right, you can say more with less number of words.

Once Again: Less Is More

It doesn't matter whether you are talking (or writing) words, phrases, sentences, paragraphs, memos, letters or reports; less is more!

Not	But
subsequently	later
forward	send
reveal	show
modification	change

Phrases:

Not	But
basic fundamentals	fundamentals
assemble together	assemble
at an early date	soon
held a meeting with	met

Not	But
What is the receptivity of the organisation to change?	Can the organisation change?
Business failure itself is an everyday occurrence in our country.	Businesses fail frequently in India.

Writing In Today's World

We live in a world where screens dominate our time.

- Many of us sleep with our phones by the bed. (Some keep them right under their pillow.)

- We check email while we're still yawning.

- Our web browser usually has more than four tabs open. Notifications and distractions come to us all day.

- We have hundreds of TV channels and a few multiplex theatres nearby.
- We also have YouTube, where content is uploaded every minute.

We are undoubtedly facing an all-out war on our attention. Here are some ways you can win it. They all involve brevity.

While writing

- Keep your sentences compact. People don't have time to decode your flowery prose, especially in business.
- Short, punchy sentences help people stay on with you.
- Keep the paragraphs short—five-six sentences.
- The more you write, the more fluent your writing will be.

Twitter

- Make your stuff easier to re-tweet.
- Twitter has a 140-character limit. If you use only 110 or so, you'll give people room to re-tweet and thus spread your message even further.

Email

Folks living on Facebook, email messages need to fit into a smaller package. Two hundred words should be the max.

- Remember: If you need more, then it's a document or a phone call or even a face-to-face meeting, but not an email.

- Do put the actionable part once at the top and again at the bottom—we're all scanning.

YouTube

- No matter which video platform you use, make your videos two minutes or less, on an average.
- Yes, if it's a speech—it should be longer. But if it's something you want people to take home, keep it under two minutes.

Phone

- If you still use a telephone, keep the call brief. Start with an agenda.
- Write the agenda beforehand so you don't ramble.
- Be polite, but don't waste five minutes on small talk.

Voicemail

- Leave your full name, phone number and the subject of the call.
- Repeat your number once more before hanging up.

While Speaking

- Brevity is the soul of wit: Clear and complete
- Keep it lively: Avoid using passive voice
- Do not use unnecessary words
- Don't be vague

Usage For Good Communication

Colloquial usage sometimes tends to disregard grammatical rules. For example, using 'me' instead of 'I'. When asked 'Who is it?', we answer 'It's me'. This is wrong in strictly grammar terms, but no one bothers.

But in written English, 'It is "I" who is responsible for this department, not "me"'.

This, of course, involves something more than grammar—sense and meaning of the word.

'Leave me alone' instead of 'Let me alone'.

Circumlocution is to write something in a long-winded way. 'The fact that one acts in a hasty manner is bound to result in an inefficient use of one's time or goods' becomes 'Haste makes waste'.

Tips For Correct Usage

- A strong vocabulary and correct usage of grammar is the key to good writing.

- Split a sentence, take it apart, then put it together like a jigsaw puzzle. Put the pieces together to form a correct sentence. This will help you to get rid of redundant words, phrases and clauses.

- Pay attention to the various parts of speech.

WRITING AT THE WORKPLACE

Golden Rules

- Beginning—The beginning of the document should be able to foster trust, confidence and a warm feeling about your company. The treatment may vary depending on the target audience.
- Think as a salesman. Keep in mind—you are selling.
- To influence people, talk in the readers language.
- To talk his language, stop answering letters and start answering people.
- Be a letter detective to answer people.
- Form the habit of studying each enquiry for clues to the written nature and personality.
- Transport—form a picture of the writer.
- Write as if you are writing to a friend.
- While answering formal letters, dig a little deeper—consider his interests.
- Make an effort to explain your business/work, if it would be beneficial for the reader.

BUSINESS WRITING TIPS

Imaginary Conversation With The Reader

If you are writing to announce a meeting, imagine telling someone face-to-face about it. List all the questions your reader may have.

- Why are we meeting?
- When is the meeting?
- Where is it?
- What's the agenda?
- Who will be there?
- Do I have to attend? What if I can't?
- Do I need to prepare? How? What?

Now, consider the order in which these questions may be asked. If you have listed the questions in a different order, rearrange them to meet your reader's needs.

Now, one by one, write the answers to these questions. Here are a few examples.

- Why are we meeting?

    We are meeting to decide whether...
- When is it?

    The meeting has been scheduled for Monday, 27 April at 2 p.m. for no more than forty-five minutes.

When you have finished organising, you have finished writing! Just edit, proofread and send.

Be Positive!

State what to do, not what to avoid.

Yes: Always process orders within two days.

No: Never take more than two days to process an order.

Say what you can do, not what you can't.

Yes: We can meet; first thing—Monday morning.

No: We can't meet now. It has to wait until Monday morning.

Use neutral rather than blaming language.

Yes: Let me clarify what I meant.

No: You misunderstood what I said.

Use words that create a positive feeling.

Yes: At this company, we value natural resources.

No: At this company, we don't waste natural resources.

Take every opportunity to communicate positively.

Yes: Thank you for your letter.

No: We have received your letter.

Know Where Passive Verbs Belong

Be careful to avoid passive voice. Rewrite the sentence using an active voice verb. For example:

- 'Your gift is appreciated' (passive) becomes 'We appreciate your gift' (active)
- '...is appreciated' (passive—impersonal) becomes 'We appreciate...' (active—warm).

When we make such changes, we replace vague phrases with concise, direct words/phrases.

But there are places where passive verbs fit just right.

- When you don't know who performed the action.

    Passive: Her car was stolen twice.

    Not: Someone stole her car twice.

- When it doesn't matter who performed the action.

    Passive: The logs are pre-cut.

    Not: A worker pre-cuts the logs.

- When we want to avoid blaming someone.

Passive: The books were lost.
Not: Derek lost the books.
- When we want to soften a directive.
Passive: This paragraph could be shortened.
Not: Shorten this paragraph.

Do More With Less!

*For over a decade, the message at work has been:
Do more with less!*

We can be much more efficient if we use fewer words. By removing an extra word, we cut down on both writing and reading time.

The paragraph below contains seventy words.

This document is for the purpose of giving the reader a detailed explanation of the inventory process. It describes the activities we currently do in a majority of instances on a daily and weekly basis. In order to provide an introduction to the process, for employees who work on a temporary basis, we have also prepared an overview, which describes the highlights of the inventory process in just two pages.

Here is a thirty-word revision:

This document explains the inventory process in detail. It describes our daily and weekly activities. We have also prepared a two-page overview to introduce the process to temporary employees.

To lighten up your sentences, watch for heavy phrases like these:

for the purpose of	=	for
a majority of	=	most
in order to	=	to
provide an introduction	=	introduce
on a daily basis	=	daily
on a regular basis	=	routinely

It's true—we can do more with less!

Breaking The Writer's Block

Avoid getting stuck

Every now and then, a blank screen or an empty page stares at us dully. Meanwhile, the digital clock shifts through the minutes. We fidget. A number of things can help us break the writer's block. Here are a few techniques.

Imagine talking to the reader: Think about the things your reader wants or needs to know. Keeping this in mind, try to write the beginning, middle or end.

Write without censoring: While writing, do not pay much attention to the writing being good or bad. Just let the words and ideas flow. Then choose your 'keepers' and build from them.

Read what you wrote previously: Reviewing some of your past works makes you feel proud. This tends to build your confidence and may give you fresh ideas.

Talk to co-workers: Don't wait to talk to your co-workers about your struggles until you're done with it.

Know what's coming! For a project that takes several sittings, end a sitting knowing what comes next and make a note of it. That way, you won't face a mental block when you begin the next time.

Take a break: This includes a change of scenery or shift to another activity.

BUSINESS LETTERS

Virtue

Make your letters pleasant.

Prompt

Always reply at once. Delay often means muddle.

Literate

Show that you have mastered the essentials of accidence, syntax and punctuation etc. Always, make a rough draft first.

Easy To Read

Pay attention to spacing; make good margins and reasonably short paragraphs.

Accurate

Pay close attention to details pertaining to time, place and quantity etc. Get the addresses and dates right. Don't over-abbreviate.

Short And Straight-forward

Keep your sentences short and to the point. Don't ramble. Conciseness is essential.

Appropriate

Bear in mind who your correspondent is. Adapt each letter to the needs of the recipient. It is better to be a foot too formal than an inch too familiar.

Natural

Be sincere and avoid jargon. Avoid exaggerated flattery or servility in letters to superiors.

Tactful

Always be willing to admit a mistake. Cultivate politeness and courtesy, and avoid sarcasm and rudeness. Even when the necessity arises for writing a 'strong' letter, remember that the iron hand is just as effective in the velvet glove.

BUSINESS WRITING SKILLS

Writing Plan And Writing

This helps you stay focused and relevant and ultimately, saves you time for writing.

Say why you are writing in the first sentence

Help your reader understand why you are writing by starting with an objective sentence.

Keep it short and simple

Don't make your reader wade through long, rambling sentences. Avoid falling into the trap of using over-formal words such as 'hereby' and 'herewith'. They will make you sound old-fashioned and pompous and don't add any meaning to your sentence. Link your ideas. Guide your reader through the text by using linking words and phrases. Words such as 'and', 'because' or 'however'; make your text flow and prevent your sentences from appearing isolated from each other.

Get the tone right

The tone of your text is the 'voice' that you use with your reader, and the one you choose depends on who you are writing to and why you are writing.

Keep your style appropriate and consistent

Bear in mind the formality of the situation.

End your correspondence by referring back to the reader.

Make sure your reader knows what the next step is. If you are asking for help in an email, you could end 'Thanks for your help'. In a letter you could write, 'I look forward to hearing from you.'

Make sure your salutation and ending are correct

If you start a letter with 'Dear Mr X' or 'Dear Ms X', end with 'Yours sincerely'. If you know your reader quite well, you can start with 'Dear' and end with 'Best wishes' or 'Best/Kind regards'. If you don't know the name of the person you are writing to and start with 'Dear Sir or Madam', end with 'Yours faithfully' rather than 'Yours sincerely'.

You can also start and end emails in the same way as letters. But if you are writing to more than one person, you can omit the salutation completely and start with your objective. Otherwise, you can end emails by writing 'Thanks' or 'Cheers', but never 'Bye'.

Pay attention to your punctuation

Most common mistakes are made with capital letters, commas and apostrophes. Remember that commas are used in lists, and to separate clauses, to give a kind of 'breathing space'. Capital letters should be used for proper nouns and to begin a new sentence. Apostrophes are used to show possession or contraction, but never for plurals.

Edit Your Writing

Read through what you have written to check for spelling and grammatical errors.

WRITING THE MINUTES OF A MEETING

Role of Minutes

- To keep people informed of the progress of projects/tasks/issues

- To remind people of what they should do and by when should it be completed
- To be a legal record of decisions

Types Of Minutes

- A verbatim record of what everyone said
- An outline of the discussion and any decisions and action points
- A brief outline of what was discussed and decisions and action points
- Only decisions and action points
- Only decisions
- Only action points

Writing Minutes

Write minutes in the past tense. You are writing about something that has already happened. When you are typing the minutes from your notes, you are recording a past event.

Mishra **stated** that staff **needed** new uniforms. (correct)

Mishra states that staff **need** new uniforms. (incorrect)

Note: Though minutes should ideally be written in the past tense, it is not mandatory to do so.

Sujit expressed concern about customer service standards. (Active voice—You are identifying specific person and what he said.) You may also say. Concern was expressed about customer service standards. (Passive voice—You are deliberately not saying who expressed the concern.)

In order to get the minutes right, one must prepare for the meeting. Here are a few things to do.

- Get a copy of the agenda.
- Find out the meaning of the terms that you don't understand.
- Read the documents that will be tabled at the meeting.

Tips for writing minutes efficiently

- Have a template for writing notes. You could use the columns 'speaker', 'item' and 'action'.
- Leave blank space to return to, if necessary.
- Interrupt if you didn't catch something.
- Be prepared to review and summarise.
- Turn the notes into minutes.
- Be accurate, brief and clear.
- Follow the order of the agenda.
- Highlight actions required.

WRITING A MEMO

Memo (short for memorandum) is a business-oriented document that is best suited for inter-office or inter-colleague correspondence. More informal in tone and organisation than a letter, memos are generally used to provide or ask for information, announce a new policy, update on personnel transfers, or for any other internal issues.

Elements Of An Effective Memo

- Grabs the reader's attention

- Provides information, makes a recommendation, or asks for action
- Supports your position or explains benefits to the reader
- Mentions the next steps and deadlines

Always take this four-step approach to writing.

Plan what you want to say

Write a draft

Revise the draft

Edit

Types Of Memos

There are four types of memos you might have to write—each with its own organisational format.

Information memo

- Used to deliver/request information or assistance
- First paragraph provides the main idea
- Second paragraph expands on the details
- Third paragraph outlines the action required

Problem-solving memo

- Suggests a specific action to improve a situation
- First paragraph states the problem
- Second paragraph analyses the problem
- Third paragraph makes a recommendation
- While making a recommendation, include positive details

Persuasion memo

- Used to encourage the reader to undertake an action
- First paragraph begins with an agreeable point
- Second paragraph introduces the idea
- Third paragraph states the benefits to the reader
- Fourth paragraph outlines the action required
- Fifth paragraph is concluded with a call to action

Internal memo proposal

- Used to convey suggestions to senior management
- First paragraph states reason for writing the memo
- Second paragraph outlines the present situation and states the writer's proposal
- Third paragraph describes advantage(s)
- Fourth paragraph mentions and diffuses disadvantage(s)
- Fifth paragraph is concluded with a call to action

Memo Parts

More informal in appearance and tone than a letter, a memo is set up in a special format. Headings, lists, tables or graphs are often used to make the information more readable. All memos consist of two sections: the heading and the body. The heading indicates who is writing to whom, when and why. The heading should include these parts.

To

- Lists the names of everyone who will receive the memo

- Includes the first and last names and titles or departments of the recipients for formal memos, memos to superiors, or if people on the list do not know each other
- If all recipients know each other's names and positions, use the initial and last name of each recipient; the names can be listed by rank, department or alphabetically
- If it is not possible to fit all the names in the 'To' area, use the phrase 'See distribution list'
- At the end of the memo, add the word 'Distribution' and then list the names of the people who will receive a copy of the memo; names can be arranged according to rank, department or alphabetically

From

- Lists the name of the writer(s) in the same way as the name(s) of the recipient(s)
- There is no complimentary close or signature line, but authors initial their names on the 'From' line

Date

- Give the month, date and year the memo is written
- Do not use abbreviations
- Avoid using numbers for months and days

Re or subject

- Indicates the main subject of the letter
- Should be as specific and concise as possible

Cc or bcc

- Lists the names of those readers who should have a copy of the memo for their information or reference but are not expected to carry out the same action as the recipients listed in the 'To' line
- 'cc' can also be placed at the end of the memo, below the distribution list (if used)

The body of a memo conveys the message and generally consists of four parts.

- **Introduction** states the general problem or main idea.
- **Statement of facts** states facts or discusses the problem(s) or issue(s).
- **Argument** explains the importance or relevance of the facts.
- **Conclusion** summarises the main idea, suggests or requests action. Memos do not have a complimentary close or signature line. Memos end with a call to action.

WRITING AN EMAIL

Email is a medium which has revolutionised the way in which we communicate with each other. In particular it is important to consider:

- Why you are using email
- The ways in which emails differ from letters and telephone conversations depends on:
  - how the email is 'topped and tailed'
  - the structure of the email

- how the attachments are used
  - how an email is formatted
- How to use emails as effectively as possible. This involves:
  - perspective
  - reflection
  - response
  - organisation
- Email etiquette include paying attention to:
  - formality
  - formatting
  - flaming
  - emoticons
  - initialises

Basics

The advent of email has revolutionised business and personal communication.

Emails inhabit a space somewhere between personal meetings, telephones and letters. It has the advantages of each of these means of communication. For instance, they are instant and direct, like face-to-face meetings, and allow a number of people to participate. They are quick and inexpensive, like telephone calls. They allow those involved to keep a permanent record of messages sent and received, like letters. But once sent, you cannot monitor the recipient's reaction to your message and then modify your message;

when you receive a message you may misjudge the sender's tone, because you have only words on the screen to go by. Another advantage of emails is that they are quick to send. However, as in a face-to-face or telephone conversation, it is easy to say something that we may regret. By contrast, letters take longer to compose and seem to allow more time for reflection before being sent.

Topping and tailing matters. It includes:

- Structure
- Attachments
- Formatting

Topping and tailing

When you compose an email, you have to consider the frame within which your message is set. This consists of a number of elements.

Structure: As we've seen, an email can vary in length from one word to thousands. Short emails are often relaxed, informal and unstructured, but longer messages usually need a clear structure.

Attachments: If the message is long, you may prefer to write it as a separate document and attach it to a covering email. Attaching separate documents has a number of advantages.

Formatting: Email usually works in plain text mode. This means that usually you cannot use formatting features, such as bold and italic text, different fonts and font sizes.

Email Etiquette

Email does encourage a more relaxed way of writing than other more traditional forms of communication. Nevertheless, a number of conventions have been established, which are often referred to as email etiquette.

Salutation and formality

Like any form of communication, the salutation depends on the way you see your relationship with the other person.

Formatting

Even in plain text email, it is possible to indicate emphasis. The most obvious way is to write in capital letters. This is like raising your voice; it should only be used very sparingly, otherwise it is simply irritating. Another way of emphasising a word or phrases is to put it in inverted commas, for instance, 'This is very disappointing.' Titles of books and films etc., can be underlined.

Emotions

It is easy to respond over-emotionally to an email. This phenomenon is sometimes referred to as 'flaming'. It can be avoided in the ways already suggested—taking time to reflect, not sending messages off straight-away, etc. You should also do everything you can to avoid your message being ambiguous. Jokes and irony can be very tricky when composing an email.

Another method that some people use when corresponding with people, whom they know well, is to use emoticons—a combination of punctuation and letters that draw faces.

Some people like using these, others hate them. Never use them in formal emails, though.

REPLYING TO EMAILS

Don't break the thread

When replying to a message, select 'Reply', rather than creating a new message; this would ensure that the thread of messages on a single subject can be kept together.

Whom to reply to: In general, it is better not to 'Reply to all' unless there is a good reason for doing so. Work groups often set up their own rules on this.

When to reply: Emails are a rapid form of communication. But the sender is never entirely sure if they have been received. Thus, it is helpful to reply promptly, even if only with a one-liner acknowledging receipt and promising to answer more fully later.

Quoting in the reply: Another thing that bulks out emails unnecessarily is the habit of copying the whole of the message you have received in your reply. Some email users do this by default, but it is usually possible to organise things so that the programme copies only those parts that you want it to. Doing this can be very useful, especially if you have been asked a number of questions; you can follow each copied question with your answer.

Cc or Bcc: Any email address you put in the 'Cc' slot can be read by all the people to whom you send the email. If you are sending a round robin message to a number of people who do not need to know each other's contact details, then you should put their email addresses in the 'Bcc' slot.

Forwarding: You may wish to forward a message that you have received to someone else to whom it was not originally sent. There are a couple of things to remember here. The sender may not have wished anyone else but you to see the message at this stage, so it is only courteous to ask permission before forwarding it. Strictly speaking, all messages are the copyright of the person who sent the mail so copying someone without permission is a breach of the copyright law. Forwarding emails is a normal practice within organisations or amongst other groups where there is a clear common goal and forwarding is expected by those concerned.

Tips for Composing Clear, Concise and Responsive Emails

- Determine the desired outcome.
- Answer: 'What's the point?'
- State benefits clearly.
- Remember: KISS—Keep it short and simple.
- Save the whole story—stick to the facts.
- Pretend as if you are in a face-to-face meeting and then write.
- Avoid excessive compliments.
- Be personal and personable.
- Make it easy to be found.
- Use simple language.

- Font and formatting matters.
- Minimise questions

Netiquette Tips

- Make sure your email includes a courteous greeting and closing. This helps to make your email not seem demanding or terse.
- Address your contact with the appropriate level of formality and make sure you spell their name correctly.
- Do a spell check. Emails with typos are not taken seriously.
- Read your email out loud to ensure that the tone is one which you desire. Try to avoid relying on formatting for emphasis; choose words that reflect your meaning. Addition of words such as 'please' and 'thank you' go a long way!
- Be sure you include all relevant details or information necessary to understand your request or point of view. Generalities may cause confusion.
- Are you using proper sentence structure? First word capitalised with appropriate punctuation? Multiple instances of '!!!' or '???' are perceived as rude or condescending.
- If your email is emotionally charged, walk away from the computer and review to reply. Review the sender's email again and be sure that you are not reading into anything that simply isn't there.

- If sending attachments, did you first ask when would be the best time to send? Did you check the file size to make sure you don't fill the receiver's inbox causing all subsequent email, to bounce?
- Refrain from using the 'Reply to all' feature to give your opinion to those who may not be interested. In most cases, replying to the sender alone is your best course of action.
- Make one last check that the address or addresses in the 'To' field are those you wish to reply to.
- Be sure that your name is reflected properly.
- Type complete sentences. Random phrases or cryptic thoughts do not lend to clear communication.
- Never assume the intent of an email. If you are not sure, 'ask' to avoid unnecessary misunderstandings.
- Just because someone doesn't ask for a response, doesn't mean you ignore them. Always acknowledge emails from those you know in a timely manner.
- Be sure that the 'Subject' field accurately reflects the content of your email.
- Don't hesitate to say, 'Thank you', 'How are you?' or 'Appreciate your help!'
- Keep emails brief and to the point. Save long conversations for the telephone.
- Always end your emails with 'Thank you,' 'Sincerely' and 'Best regards'.

Formatting Emails

Do not type in all caps. That's yelling or reflects shouting; it is called 'SCREAM' in the Internet jargon.

- If you bold type, know that you are bolding your statement and it will be taken that way by the other side.
- Do not use patterned backgrounds. It makes your email harder to read.
- Stay away from fancy fonts.
- Use emoticons sparingly to ensure your tone and intent are clear.
- Typing your emails in all lowercase gives the perception of lack of education or laziness.
- Refrain from using multiple font colours in one email. It makes your email harder to view and can lead to your intent being misinterpreted.
- Use formatting sparingly. Instead try to rely on choosing the most accurate words to reflect your tone and avoid misunderstandings.

Email Attachments

- When sending large attachments, always 'zip' or compress them before sending.
- Never send large attachments without notice! Always first ask what would be the best time to send them.
- Never open an attachment from someone you don't know.
- Be sure your virus and spyware programmes are up to date and include scanning of your emails and attachments both incoming and outgoing.

- It is better to spread multiple attachments over several emails rather than attaching them all to one email to avoid clogging.
- Make sure that the other side has the same software as you before sending attachments or they may not be able to open it.

Forwarding Emails

- Don't forward emails that ask you to do so—no matter how noble the cause may be—don't. Most are hoaxes.
- If someone asks you to refrain from forwarding emails, they have that right and you shouldn't get mad or take it personally.
- When forwarding an email, if you cannot take the time to type a personal comment to the person you are forwarding it to, then don't bother.
- Don't forward anything without editing all the forwarding '>>>>', other email addresses headers etc., from all the other forwarders.
- Be careful when forwarding emails on political or controversial issues. The recipient may not appreciate it.

Business Emails

- Think of your business email as though it is on your business letterhead and you'll never go wrong!
- If you cannot respond to an email promptly, at the very least, reply to confirm receipt and indicate when the sender can expect your response.

- Emailing site owners about your product or service through the site form is still spam. First, ask them if they want more information.
- When replying to emails, always respond promptly and edit unnecessary information from the post you are responding to.
- Formality reflects respect. Maintain the highest level of formality with new email contacts until the relationship warrants otherwise. Refrain from getting too informal too soon in your email communications.
- Never send anyone an email they need to unsubscribe from, especially if they didn't subscribe to it in the first place!
- Be very careful about how you use 'Reply to all' and 'Cc' in a business environment.
- Never send business attachments outside of business hours and confirm the format in which the attachment can be sent.

IM, BlackBerry

- With Instant Messaging (IM) and Chat, try not to be overly cryptic or the meaning can be misread.
- Use IM for casual topics or informational briefs. It is not appropriate for serious topics or confrontational issues.
- Always start by asking if the person you are IMing is available and if it is a good time to chat. Refrain from IMing during meetings or when you need to focus.

- Practice communicating briefly and succinctly.
- IMing is not an excuse to forget your grade school education.
- If you are not a smooth multi-tasker, do not engage in multiple IM sessions and leave someone hanging while you communicate with another person.
- Learn how to use the features of your IM programme, especially the 'busy' and 'away' features.
- Never IM under an alias to take a peek at friends' or associates' activities.
- Take into consideration who you are communicating with to determine the acronyms and emoticons that should be used, if at all.
- Type unto others as you would have them type unto you.

WRITING A SPEECH

Here are a few tips on how to write a memorable speech.

Prepare Early

Begin gathering material for your speech right away. As you learn more about your topic, new ideas for writing and organising it, will automatically come to you.

Be Audience-Centred

Everything you write should be aligned with the needs of the audience. Aim all your efforts at helping the audience understand what you are saying.

Start At The End, First

Write the conclusion of your talk right away. Decide what you want the audience to do or think as a result of your speech. Then write the speech using that as a guide.

Write For The Ear, Not The Eye

Experienced writers know that every medium and project have their own language, cadence, style and structure. Don't write the speech to be read. You need to write your speech in a way that when your audience hears it, they get it.

Make Rough Drafts First And Polish Later

Don't pressure yourself by trying to write the perfect speech at the outset. The best speeches come only after many, many rewrites.

Put Your Own Spin On The Material

You may block your creative juices if you think everything you say has to be original. Don't worry about being unique, just put your personal spin on it. The audience wants to hear your personal point of view.

Make Only Three Main Points

It is always tempting to tell as much as you can about a subject, but this will confuse and overwhelm your audience. Stick to three key points and your audience will find it easier to follow your speech.

Craft A Take-Away Line

When people can't make it to a speaker's session, they ask

others who were there, 'What did the speaker talk about?' and 'What was the speaker's take-away line?' You'd like people to walk out with that nugget.

Decide The Minimum Your Audience Needs To Know

What is the very least the audience needs to know about your topic? What is the most critical? Leave out the material that would be 'nice to know'; stick to what is important. You probably won't have time for it anyhow.

Use The 'What Is In It For Me' Principle

People are only interested in material that concerns them.

Note:

- Write as if you are conversing with a person.
- Decide what you want your audience to do or think differently as a result of your speech.
- Use 'Audience-involvement' devices.

Listening Skills

Healthy listening requires more than just hearing.

> **Listening For Understanding**
> - Avoid judging or drawing conclusions before you have all the information.
> - Recognise what situations call for selective listening and what situations would benefit from compassionate listening.
> - Evaluate verbal messages as well as body language; note conflicting messages.
> - Listen actively and make eye contact.
> - Don't be afraid to show some emotion in response to what is being said.
> - Ask for feedback from the speaker about whether or not you have understood what they have communicated.
> - Note what information is left out.

ADVANTAGES OF BEING A GOOD LISTENER

Here are a few advantages of being a good listener.
- Being a good listener can help you see the world through the eyes of others.

- It enriches your understanding and expands your capacity to empathise.
- It also increases your contact with the outside world by helping you improve your communication skills.
- Good listening skills can provide you with a deeper level of understanding about someone's situation and help you to know which words are best to use/avoid in a particular situation.

As simple as listening (and acknowledging) may seem, doing it well, particularly when disagreements arise, takes sincere effort and lots of practice.

Listening is not the same as hearing

Hearing	Listening
• Hearing is the ability to listen to the sounds around you; it is passive.	• Listening is a learnt skill; it is active.
• The goal of hearing is to receive verbal and non-verbal messages; we do it without thinking.	• Understanding is the goal of listening.

TYPES OF LISTENING

Discriminative Listening

It develops at an early stage in one's mother's womb; child can distinguish the father's voice from that of the mother. Basic listening does not involve understanding of the meanings of words or phrases.

At an airport: One can distinguish the voices of male/female and old/young. Though one may not understand what is being said, but the tone, mannerism and voice give some idea.

Comprehensive Listening

Comprehensive listening involves understanding the message. For this, the listener first needs appropriate vocabulary and language skills. Using overly complicated language or technical jargon can, therefore, be a barrier to comprehensive listening.

It is further complicated by the fact that two different people listening to the same thing may understand the message in two different ways. This problem can be multiplied in a group setting, like a classroom. Non-verbal signals can greatly aid communication and comprehension.

Specific Listening Types

Discriminative and comprehensive listening are prerequisites for specific listening types. Listening types can be defined on the basis of the goal that is to be achieved from listening.

The three most common types of listening in interpersonal relationships are: Informational, Critical and Therapeutic (I-C-T):

- Informational (listening to learn)
- Critical (listening to evaluate and analyse)
- Therapeutic or empathetic (listening to understand feeling and emotion)

In reality, you may have more than one goal for listening at any given time, for instance, you may be listening to learn while attempting to be empathetic. Empathy is the ability to understand and share the feelings of another person.

Informational listening

Whenever you listen to learn something, you are engaged in informational listening. This is true in many day-to-day situations—in education and at work; when you listen to news or watching a documentary; when a friend tells you a recipe; or when you are talked-through a technical problem with a computer—there are many other examples of informational listening.

Informational listening, especially in formal settings like in official meetings or while in an educational institution, is often accompanied by note taking—a way of recording key information so that it can be reviewed later.

Critical listening

We can be said to be engaged in critical listening when the goal is to evaluate or scrutinise what is being said. Critical listening is a much more active behaviour than informational listening and usually involves some sort of problem-solving or decision-making.

Critical listening is akin to critical reading—both involve analysis of the information being received and alignment with what we already know or believe.

While informational listening may be mostly concerned with receiving facts and/or new information, critical listening is about analysing opinion and making a judgement.

When the word 'critical' is used to describe listening, reading or thinking, it does not necessarily mean that you are claiming that the information you are listening to is somehow faulty or flawed. Rather, critical listening means engaging in what you are listening to by asking yourself 'what is the speaker trying to say?', 'What is the main argument being presented?' and 'How does what I'm hearing differ from my beliefs, knowledge or opinion?'

Critical listening is, therefore, fundamental to true learning. It is often important, when listening critically, to have an open mind and not be biased or influenced by stereotypes or preconceived ideas. By doing this, you will become a better listener and broaden your knowledge and perception of other people and your relationships with them.

Therapeutic or empathetic listening

Empathetic listening involves attempting to understand the feelings and emotions of the speaker—to put yourself into the speaker's shoes and share their thoughts.

Empathy is not the same as sympathy; it involves more than being compassionate or feeling sorry for somebody. It involves a deeper connection—a realisation and understanding of another person's point of view.

This type of listening does not involve making judgements or offering advice, but gently encouraging the speaker to explain and elaborate on their feelings and emotions.

Other Listening Types

Although usually less important or useful in interpersonal relationships, there are other types of listening that we engage in.

Appreciative listening

Appreciative listening is listening for enjoyment. A good example is listening to music, especially as a way to relax.

Rapport listening

When trying to build rapport with others, we can engage in a type of listening that encourages the other person to trust and like us.

Selective listening

This is a more negative type of listening, it implies that the listener is somehow biased towards what is being said. Bias can be due to preconceived ideas or emotionally difficult communication. Selective listening is a sign of failing communication.

PERFECT APPRAISAL

Performance appraisal is the process of evaluating and documenting one's performance on the job. It is part of career development. *Perfect Appraisal* deals with:

- Appraisal process
- Training for appraisal
- Pitfalls in appraisals
- Dos and don'ts of appraisal

Perfect Appraisal provides simple techniques to a perfect appraisal with a holistic approach.

PERFECT ASSERTIVENESS

Assertiveness is important in all forms of communication. It is a way of relating to others that respects both your own and other people's needs, wants and rights. Aggressiveness provokes counter-aggression, assertiveness doesn't. *Perfect Assertiveness* spells out:

- Assertiveness training
- Responses: Passive, aggressive and assertive
- Effective communication
- Assertiveness skills
- Benefits of being assertive

Perfect Assertiveness helps you understand assertiveness as a life skill.

PERFECT CV

A curriculum vitae (CV) or résumé presents a record of your qualities, skills and experience to an employer, so that your suitability for a particular job can be assessed. In Latin, 'curriculum vitae' means 'the way your life has run' and 'résumé' is the French word for 'summary'. *Perfect CV* deals with:

- Making a CV special
- Writing a CV with lack of experience
- Tailoring a CV
- Digital CVs
- Online CVs

Perfect CV helps you to compile your CV and suggests ways to improve it.

PERFECT LEADER

If you want to inspire, motivate and engage, and move people into action, leadership is the ability you require. Leaders set direction and develop the skill to guide people to the right destination. *Perfect Leader* spells out:

- Leadership styles
- Initiatives that are needed
- Proactive tools
- The importance of perseverance
- Methods to step out of the comfort zone

Perfect Leader helps you to inspire the vision of the future as a leader. It equips you to make strategic decisions, shape conflict and find your competitive edge.

PERFECT MEETING

Meetings help one to build rapport. They are a forum for inter-learning and understanding; a platform to share information. *Perfect Meeting* is about the basic skills of management. It deals with:

- Effective meetings
- Conference meetings
- Stand-up meetings
- One-on-one meetings
- Tasks and skills of the chairperson

Perfect Meeting helps you generate cooperation and commitment to attain higher levels of performance.

PERFECT NEGOTIATION

In order to settle differences, one needs to master the skill of negotiation. Without this skill, conflicts and disagreements will arise. *Perfect Negotiation* deals with the process of negotiation and its different stages.

- Preparation
- Discussion
- Goals
- Win-win outcome
- Agreement

Perfect Negotiation helps you master the different types of negotiation formats, styles, and preparing strategies for negotiation.

PERFECT PRESENTATION

Presentation skills are critical as they help one to inform, motivate and inspire others. It is a means to get a message across to the listeners, with a persuasive element. *Perfect Presentation* talks about:

- Canons of persuasive presentations
- Verbal communication
- Non-verbal communication
- Styles of presentation
- Opening and closing of a presentation

Perfect Presentation helps you master the art of making effective presentations.